SOS AMERICA: PLEASE READ THIS BEFORE YOU VOTE!

Gregg Powers

iUniverse, Inc.
New York   Bloomington

SOS America: Please Read This Before You Vote!

Copyright © 2008 by Gregg Powers

iUniverse books may be ordered through booksellers or by contacting:

iUniverse
1663 Liberty Drive
Bloomington, IN 47403
www.iuniverse.com
1-800-Authors (1-800-288-4677)

Because of the dynamic nature of the Internet, any Web addresses or links contained in this book may have changed since publication and may no longer be valid. The views expressed in this work are solely those of the author and do not necessarily reflect the views of the publisher, and the publisher hereby disclaims any responsibility for them.

ISBN: 978-0-595-49373-9 (pbk)
ISBN: 978-0-595-61074-7 (ebk)

Printed in the United States of America

SOS America: Please Read This Before You Vote!

Gregg Powers

iUniverse, Inc.
New York   Bloomington

SOS America: Please Read This Before You Vote!

Copyright © 2008 by Gregg Powers

iUniverse books may be ordered through booksellers or by contacting:

iUniverse
1663 Liberty Drive
Bloomington, IN 47403
www.iuniverse.com
1-800-Authors (1-800-288-4677)

Because of the dynamic nature of the Internet, any Web addresses or links contained in this book may have changed since publication and may no longer be valid. The views expressed in this work are solely those of the author and do not necessarily reflect the views of the publisher, and the publisher hereby disclaims any responsibility for them.

ISBN: 978-0-595-49373-9 (pbk)
ISBN: 978-0-595-61074-7 (ebk)

Printed in the United States of America

PREFACE

This book is not a political book designed to influence you to vote for any specific party or any given candidate in the 2008 election or future elections. Indeed, this book is designed to be a wake-up call for the United States before it is too late. We, the American public, are responsible for those we vote into office, and if we vote for those without the moral compass to do what is right, then their failures will be our failures, and the resulting disaster will then be on our own heads. Please consider the message of this book as you contemplate your vote for your leaders, your representatives, and your judges, regardless of the level of the office for which they are running.

My only motivation in presenting the concepts in this book is to call this country to return to its roots and abandon the dangerous direction in which it continues to head. I only intend to acknowledge God's way as right and to encourage those who claim to be followers of God to vote for candidates who espouse positions that are as consistent with God's commands as possible.

I have no financial motives, as the profits from this book will be fully distributed to those who help others in need and who make God's will known to others, as well as to those who are helping to call this nation back to its roots.

The concepts in this book are not something that I created; the message I share with you here is not for my glory but for the glory of God and the best interests of our country. I am simply depicting the relationship between our responsibilities, as followers of the one true God, and our responsibilities as citizens in a democracy.

I stand in awe of those who have seen their property confiscated, endure persecution, and even given their lives of themselves and their families all because they do nothing but share the truth of God. These people are making the ultimate sacrifice so that others can come to know God's will and the sacrifice undertaken by Jesus on their behalf. It is these people who have abandoned all selfish and worldly motives in order to share God's love and his commands. We will not debate their sacrifice here but will only say that it mirrors the sacrifice of their savior Jesus, and they are doing this without any earthly reward.

Although the level of persecution in the United States has not yet reached the level of persecution in many other places in the world, we are heading that way. Imagine a time in the United States when those who simply speak the truth of God would be killed for doing so by those who seek to protect their own selfish motives.

There are many who espouse their own agenda, opposing the one true God, doing so for their own glory, their own selfishness, and their own benefit. They do so because they are unwilling to acknowledge God's way as correct, but they are fully willing to assert the superiority of their moral values, which in reality are often immoral. Yet even though they believe they have the right to override God's values, they deny the same rights to other human beings who disagree with their values, resulting in the ultimate hypocrisy.

Those who are committed to opposing God have no problem lying or doing whatever is necessary to try to pull others into their rebellion against God. A primary example of this is the fallacious claim of "separation of church and state," which is historically inaccurate. We, the people of this country, must stand up for what is right, according to God's standard, or be swept away with those who oppose God.

Finally, although the love of God is deep, God has shown time and time again that he will not put up with disobedience forever, especially intentional disobedience. This book in no way demeans God's love in *any* manner; indeed, it is one of the defining attributes of God, and it's only through his love and mercy that he has not punished me more extensively for my sins. There are prices to be paid for sin, however, yet our primary motivation for avoiding sin should be our love for God, knowing him to be all powerful.

And so I ask you: is there a motive here other than spreading the message of God's commands and God's will so that this country can return to what has made it great? As you read this, ask yourselves what motivations there might be, other than getting this country refocused on the commands of our Creator and acknowledging his way — and his way alone — as right. Then ask yourself what the motivations are of those in this country who are leading us away from God. It is time, my fellow countrymen and countrywomen, to take a stand for the God of the Bible, who has blessed our country and us as individuals for so long.

Finally, I would like to thank both Lisa Partch and David Lehti for their invaluable contributions to this book. They have been good friends and inestimable advisors as these concepts have been developed and presented. May God bless them and their hearts.

Introduction

Fellow countrymen and countrywomen, I love what this country has traditionally stood for: helping others throughout the world, trying to do what is right according to God's standard, the willingness of our military personnel to sacrifice themselves for others' safety and freedom, and an adherence to the values of purity, modesty, and humility. Because of these values, we have traditionally been a great and blessed country. But what has made America great?

- Does America have the largest population?

- Are Americans smarter than other nationalities?

- Are Americans more talented?

- Does America have more natural resources?

- Does America have more geographical territory?

- Has America traditionally had more liberal laws?

The obvious answer to each of these questions is no. Yet there is something unique about America. Most would agree that America has been blessed to a greater degree than other nations on this earth, well beyond its human and natural resources. Upon careful review, one thing is dramatically different in America from other nations in the world and perhaps in the history of all nations. As much as people may have trouble accepting it, the major difference is in the belief system held by the Founding Fathers, which has guided our government until recently and is represented in the documents that founded America.

I invite each of you to consider the following quotes taken directly from founding documents, which refute those who claim separation of church and state. (the key words for consideration have been Italicized):

"When in the Course of human events, it becomes necessary for one people to dissolve the political bands which have connected them with another, and to assume among the powers of the earth, the separate and equal station to which the *Laws of Nature and of Nature's God* entitle them, a decent respect to the opinions of mankind requires that they should declare the causes which impel them to the separation.

"We hold these truths to be self-evident, that all men are created equal, that they are *endowed by their Creator* with certain unalienable rights that among these are Life, Liberty and the pursuit of Happiness."

"And for the support of this Declaration, *with a firm reliance on the protection of divine providence*, we mutually pledge to each other our Lives, our Fortunes and our sacred Honor."

It is important to note that the rights we enjoy as Americans do not come from the government; instead, these rights "are endowed by our Creator," so these rights can never be taken away by the government.

The words of the "Battle Hymn of the Republic" accentuate God throughout the chorus: "Our God is marching on" — yes, the God of the Bible.

America's Founding Fathers held to a Christian belief system that helped guide them in creating America.

America's Founding Fathers were focused on creating "One nation, under God," whose primary purpose was to honor God. In this year 2008, America has 232 years of history that document God's blessings. We Americans cannot take credit for our success; we were not born smarter, we are not more talented, and we do not possess more natural resources.

America has been greatly blessed by God because of our history in trying to submit to him and his commands, and this reason — and this reason alone — is the *only* reason we have been so blessed!

There is other evidence of the intentions of the Founding Fathers and our country's subsequent leaders, which have been warped by those who are dedicated to opposing God. Consider the following:

- As you walk up the steps of the building that houses the U.S. Supreme Court, you can see, in a frieze near the top of the building, a sculpture that depicts the world's law-givers, and each one is facing someone in the middle, who is facing forward with a full frontal view. The person at the center is Moses, and he is holding the Ten Commandments!

- As you enter the Supreme Court courtroom, the two huge oak doors have the Ten Commandments engraved on the lower portion of each door.

- Inside the courtroom, on the wall right above where the Supreme Court judges sit is a display of the Ten Commandments!

- There are Bible verses etched in stone all over the federal buildings and monuments in Washington, D.C.

- James Madison, the fourth president, known as the "Father of the Constitution," made the following statement: *"We have staked the whole of all our political institutions upon the capacity of mankind for self-government, upon the capacity of each and all of us to govern ourselves, to control ourselves, to sustain ourselves according to the Ten Commandments of God."*

- Patrick Henry, that patriot and Founding Father of our country, said, *"It cannot be emphasized too strongly or too often that this great nation was founded not by religionists but by Christians, not on religions but on the Gospel of Jesus Christ."*

- Every session of Congress begins with a prayer by a paid preacher, whose salary has been paid by taxpayers since 1777.

- Fifty-two of the fifty-five founders of the Constitution were members of the established orthodox churches in the colonies.

- Thomas Jefferson worried that the courts would overstep their authority and instead of interpreting the law would begin making law, establishing an oligarchy, where a few rule over many.

- The very first Supreme Court justice, John Jay, said, *"Americans should select and prefer Christians as their rulers."*

Fellow countrymen and countrywomen, given the blessings we have enjoyed over these past 232 years, how have we gotten to the point where everything we have traditionally held near and dear to our hearts is now wrong and unconstitutional?

For the past 232 years, America has been a nation that has tried to honor God, but in the past forty-plus years, a movement has grown to remove God from America, and the country has witnessed a great deterioration of our moral fabric. As a nation, we stand at a crossroads with two paths before us. Do not be fooled; there are only two choices.

Will America remain a nation under God, or will it turn its back on him?

While some in this country still seek to follow the commands of God, we are increasingly led by those who claim to know God when they do not or by those who just do not believe in God and claim the same. Regardless of an individual's claims, evidence of whether a person knows God is based on his actions and his positions on critical issues. If an individual really follows God, they will take positions on issues that are consistent with what he teaches.

What is most amazing about this is that this country has done great things and prospered greatly during the periods when we followed God's commands and sought his will. But in not being satisfied with the blessings we have enjoyed, we have large numbers of people herding us away from God through the advocating of ungodly positions. Because we have turned away from God, we are now starting to pay the price. We will not be able to believe how bad it will get for us and those we love — and it will be our fault!

We simply must turn this country around, for if we do not, if we give in to those who advocate and practice ungodly activities, our entire society will fall, and each of us will suffer. This may seem like the comment of an alarmist, but it is not: we are headed for very hard times in this country. I implore you to consider the counsel of this book and return to following the commands of the one true God before we face the inevitable consequences of our rejection of the Lord's commands. This country simply cannot continue to make the choices it has made if we expect to emerge from this unscathed, much less be blessed by the God who has traditionally looked out for this country.

In 2 Chronicles 7:14, God makes this pledge: *"If my people, who are called by my name, will humble themselves and pray and seek my face and turn from their wicked ways, then will I hear from heaven and will forgive their sin and will heal their land."*

How many times in our history have we been saved from near destruction while the rest of the world suffers? Some see coincidence, but many of us—I myself included—see divine providence. We have been delivered from many natural disasters, experienced only a minimal number of attacks on our homeland, and have been protected from would-be world rulers. There are so many places in history that only a small change in timing, a small change in direction, a slightly different decision, or a small change in resolve would have had tremendous repercussions for the United States. Yet these did not happen because God looked after this country and guided those who sought his counsel!

Our leadership in the world is being compromised, not by things such as the Iraq War, but because we have given up many of our moral values. Many people in this country, including many of our leaders, want to continue to move even farther away from God's teachings and commands, but they do not understand the real cause of our problems, and they will end up damaging this country more than helping it.

There have been periods in our country's history when we have believed in ourselves and were able to accomplish great things. To get there again, we need to unite on the values that made this country great. These are godly values, not the ungodly selfishness that runs rampant in our country! The set of practices we have adopted as of late are rooted in our own selfishness which comes largely from refusing to submit to God's will and his commands. God has taught us self-sacrifice, not selfishness. Abortion is about selfishness, drugs are about selfishness, adultery is about selfishness, alcoholism is about selfishness, gas guzzlers are about selfishness, materialism is about selfishness, and opposing the Iraq War (believe it or not) is about selfishness. It is this ungodly selfishness — the focus on self by many — and the advocacy by those practicing selfishness, to others in this country of those same ungodly values, continue to rip this great country apart.

This selfishness is the primary cause of what is destroying this country. Some of our leaders and potential leaders play directly to our selfishness, telling us what they think we want to hear with respect to taxes, with respect to the Iraq war, and similar issues regardless of whether it is right or not. They promise us things that we want, even though they have no idea how to provide what they promise. Paul foretold of this almost two thousand years ago.

In 2 Timothy 4:3, we see: *"For the time will come when men will not put up with sound doctrine. Instead, to suit their own desires, they will gather around them a great number of teachers to say what their itching ears want to hear."*

Other countries live with so much less; we consume so much. The gluttony that America embraces, along with the ever-widening moral divide between our values and God's, is a recipe for disaster. Instead of being on our knees, thanking God, we keep looking for more ways to oppose God. If we in this country would stop focusing on our selfishness and start focusing on others, so many evils within this country would be righted.

We, as a country, are going to have to make some hard decisions with regard to what we are going to do and what we are going to be. If we are to make this a great country again, we must be willing to look to our past and to re-adopt past virtues and values. We must reject the selfishness of our constituents and our leaders. We are moving toward a more immoral and selfish society, rather than a more moral and selfless society.

While this book addresses the specific responsibilities of those who live in a democracy and are sincere about following the one true God, we must return to God in all aspects of our lives, not just in the support of political candidates. May the Lord have mercy on this country if we will not submit to his will and his standard of righteousness!

DIRE TIMES

The United States is heading in a dire direction; we have lost our way. Politicians sell out their country for money and violate both the moral law and established statutes. Our leaders recklessly spend the Social Security funds we have entrusted to them with no reasonable plan to pay it back except to print more money, further devaluing the money already in circulation. Our children are under attack in the very schools where they are supposed to be safe, and they are not even safe from abduction in their own yards. Our children plot to kill others in the schools they attend. Some children are being raised to believe that this country owes them everything and that they owe their country nothing. Video games and television, replete with violence, have become the learning staple of our youth.

There is an ever-advancing homosexual agenda, as practicing individuals try to indoctrinate our youth into these God forbidden practices under the cover of "genetics" – that individuals were created that way. The expansion of gambling across this nation is out of control. We spend thousands per year on our pets, while many children are starving around the globe. Individuals make dangerous drugs in their homes while young children look on. Abortion kills more than 1 million babies each year in this country. We spend money on incredible luxuries, when the majority of the world tries to live on less than two dollars per day. Our country is racking up debt faster than it can pay it off—we are going bankrupt.

Many of our women are under attack and fall victim to spousal abuse, abduction, and murder. Sexual slavery exists in this country because there is a demand for it. Young children are kidnapped and sexually assaulted. American men travel to Bangkok and other cities to abuse and engage in prostitution young children, who themselves have been forced into prostitution. Pornography, which can lead to assault, is rampant on the Internet because there is demand for it. "Leaders" of civil rights movements cast summary judgments of events before the facts are known, only to be proved wrong later demonstrating not their commitment to the truth, but to their agenda. We have "gangsta rap" which degrades women and incites violence. We have more and more fathers abandoning their responsibilities as parents. Some use the courts in an attempt to censure God, attempting to justify this by espousing a historically inaccurate premise of separation of church and state. Judges make up their own laws, yet they are unwilling to protect our children from predators by failing to punish the guilty who abuse the children. Just look at the recent death of Brooke Bennett allegedly killed by a sexual offender who was not in prison where they belonged because of prior crimes

Educators spend more time on issuing dissertations on their personal political views (which are largely ungodly) than on educating our children on the facts—and then are appalled when a student takes an automatic weapon and slays children and teachers. They advocate abandoning the author of morality (God) and yet cannot understand that this type of teaching leads individuals to a moral inversion, where any truth is acceptable, reaping, in time, the consequences of their teachings.

"Leaders" in Congress pander to leaders of various religions by having them say prayers to false gods as an opening to their sessions, demonstrating their inability to tell right from wrong. We cannot even enforce the immigration laws of this country, which leads us to dilute our nationality, further fractionalizing the country. We have moved from a nation of law to a nation of lawlessness. Many of our lawmakers cannot bring themselves to do what is right, preferring to submit to those peddling influence for their own personal gain.

Talk show hosts and celebrities offer all manner of ungodly advice, yet people follow them as if they themselves were gods. Because they either do not understand godly perspectives on how to deal with issues or because they are dedicated to rebellion against God's teachings, they surround themselves with people who as Paul said "tell them what their itching ears are longing to hear."

Finally, those who cannot remember history are doomed to repeat it. Many refuse to acknowledge and confront aggression believing it to be in the minds of those who do demonstrate vigilance against evil. Many show complete disdain for those who are making the ultimate sacrifice by giving their lives in trying to protect the innocent both in this country and in Iraq. Those who oppose what our brave troops are doing are being intellectually captured without firing a shot because they have bought into a naiveté believing the essence of man to be good even though history demonstrates otherwise.

Add to this the natural disasters that have recently befallen us, and we should see a pattern of warnings from God. But just as some scientists declare, in their ignorance, that there is no God—although they can neither truly understand how the universe was created or how life was formed—we will likely continue to look for every explanation for the problems in this country except for the one that is accurate: God is trying to get our attention. I find it interesting that less than one week after the State of California initiated gay marriage in opposition to the majority of voters in the state it was struck with an unprecedented series of lightning storms and is now burning with more than 800 fires. Was this part of God's response for the State of California's opposition of what God teaches? We will never know for sure, but it should at least be considered, yet many will not even question a potential connection. How many in our nation will have to lose their possessions or their loved ones before they turn back to God and cease opposing him? God has the unique capability to get our attention as no one else does. If we ignore the less severe attempts to get our attention, God may increase the suffering to a point where we will have no choice but to turn to him. This is no different than parents who are told their child is terminally ill. In such a case, it is surprising how many parents turn to God in such a situation even though they may have claimed they did not believe in God beforehand.

There is no place in the Bible that God indicates that a country must be ruled by a single type of group or individual (Christians or otherwise) or with a specific style of government, but regardless of how the country is ruled, we are all expected to adhere to God's laws (yes, this is the God of the Bible, because there is no other). It is not acceptable to worship any other God than the God of the Bible or to make any law that is inconsistent with his commands. God teaches us *not* to be tolerant of ungodly practices. Historically, Israel was punished when it accepted the ungodly practices of other nations, and so will we be punished. Even the Israelites, who did not actively pursue evil acts, were affected by their country's evil acts because they did not *actively oppose* such acts. God often demanded the destruction of other nations that routinely practiced evil acts. We had better understand who our Creator is and what his authorities and powers are.

God has blessed this nation since it was founded. Anything that we in this country have is because of his blessing, not because of our own character, military might, resources, or intelligence. These blessings are not our birthright, but they have been bestowed on us because we have always acknowledged the one true God and because we have traditionally based our laws on his commands. As our nation becomes more and more accepting of ungodly practices, as it rejects more and more of God's laws, and as we develop our own laws in conflict with God's commands, we only shorten the time to our destruction as he pulls his blessings away from us and moves this country to its worst nightmare.

I am aware that God has greater love and patience than I can even conceive, but as the Bible shows, his love and patience are not unlimited. He gives people lots of time to repent and to turn back to him, but he will act—and act decisively—when he decides it is time. We are made in his image, and just as we will not tolerate unlimited disobedience from our offspring, neither will he tolerate it from us. As a country, let us not try to see how much we can get away with. Rather, let us return to the God who has blessed us.

Let me share with you my conviction, based on what the Bible teaches. As a country, we have behaved with such evil that we should have already been destroyed. Only the depth of God's mercy has stopped this from happening. But God's mercy, although great, is not unlimited, and each time we slay a baby, free a child molester, or approve of homosexual acts, we are increasing his wrath against us as a nation. This country cannot stand without God's support! We must turn back to God not only because it is right, but also because it is he who holds our future in his hands.

This threat is real, regardless of whether we suffer at the hands of terrorists, disease, starvation, natural disasters, or other means of punishment that our Creator declares for our disobedience. We will suffer, our families will suffer, our kids will suffer, and our friends will suffer—and it will be our fault. Do not doubt this. Look at what is happening around us now and how much worse this country is getting each day. Even though the problems in this country may not have personally affected you yet, the time is coming when they will. Do not think that money or anything you have can rescue you from God's wrath if you are determined to support ungodly lifestyles and those who advocate ungodly positions on issues.

Consider the civilizations of the past that lost their moral compass. Israel did this many times, and each time it was punished. This is a matter of historical record. The people were killed by invaders, by disease, and by famine. They were subjugated by other countries. Only after the loss of many lives and extensive suffering did some of them return to God. Do we, the people of the United States, have to be so thick-headed that we test God's patience as we anger him with our actions? Do we actually have to sample God's wrath before we change? Are we so out of touch with reality that when disaster does strike, we simply write it off without even considering that this may be punishment for rejecting God?

When 9/11 occurred, the churches filled up for a short time and then, shortly thereafter, reverted to pre-9/11 levels of attendance. God is not fooled by such transient worship. One of the true tests of worshipping God is obeying him. We as a country are not only disobeying God, but we also are moving to become even more disobedient.

The devil, through the feeding of our own selfish desires, has seduced many in this country—many who call themselves Christians— into dropping their guard, convincing them not worry about things. Too many of us sit back and accept everyone and every action that is consistent with man's ever-evolving, ever-changing, and ever-escalating ungodly set of morals. Like the proverbial frog in the boiling pot, our turning away from God is happening at such a measured pace that we are accepting of it until it is too late. Others follow false religions, and still others claim that no God exists. Each of these cannot be true. Each of these deviant paths results in separation from God, so that he will not hear our prayers when we do need him. (Isaiah 59:1–2: *Surely the arm of the LORD is not too short to save, nor his ear too dull to hear. But your iniquities have separated you from your God; your sins have hidden his face from you, so that he will not hear.*)

Whether Republican, Democrat, Independent, or any other party, we must adhere to the laws of the God of the Bible if we are going to continue to be blessed. If we will not stand up for that which is right, we will be swept away with those who are committed to disobeying God.

The reason that many of our politicians can no longer get the things done for this country is that they do not agree on what is right and what is wrong. Many politicians claim to follow God, but they substitute God's commands with their own beliefs—or in some cases, the ungodly desires of their constituency. While policy-making has always been tenuous, the fact that politicians don't agree on a common standard of right and wrong makes the ability to pass laws very difficult. There is, of course, a standard for right and wrong as specified by God, but our governing authorities must be able to accept it and follow it. Many politicians are unwilling to tell us the truth either because they cannot recognize it or because they are deliberately trying to mislead us. It should speak volumes when a politician votes for a law which contradicts God's law. It should also speak volumes when a politician seeks to censure God and remove references to him in public life rather than seek to thank the God who has blessed this county.

Only recently, with gas at more than $4.00 a gallon, have our leaders started telling us that they must increase our taxes to pay the debt that we have run up. They will not tell us that we must eliminate our dependence on foreign oil. They continue to lead us toward financial oblivion as we approach bankruptcy. Add to this the extreme bi-partisanship that causes our leaders to focus more on pointing out the faults of others than on working on what we need to accomplish—no wonder we cannot get back on track. Many of our politicians see their being elected as a means of acquiring power and wealth and do not truly seek to do that which is right.

Some of those in power seek to surround themselves with others who share their warped perspectives of right and wrong. They block the appointment of judges who have sound moral values, while seeking to install judges who oppose godly values. They do this because they have established their own morality and because they reject the true author of morality. What possible reason could a person give for wanting to eliminate the Ten Commandments from school, from courts, from public places? Some claim they do not want to offend others. In reality, they cannot tell right from wrong, and so they try to eliminate the authoritative source of right and wrong. They cannot stand for the truth because they cannot recognize it. Others attempt to create their own morality, using their own values and suppressing the truth while attempting to corrupt others who do not share their morally corrupt views. They want to make their own evil practices the standard for right and wrong and censure those who would hold to the godly standard.

We have a growing dichotomy in this county between those who believe in God and make an attempt to submit to God's commands, and the group that claims to believe in God but are committed to every type of ungodly practice. They will have to answer to the Lord in the long run, but they are also ruining this country in the short term. Do not be deceived. If a person says that he or she follows God and then espouses or adopts ungodly positions on issues, then he or she is either horribly misguided, a coward, or a liar. Any of these attributes should disqualify him or her as a leader of this country. We, as the constituency, must invest the time to determine whether a candidate can make decisions consistent with God's commands—unless we want to face the consequences of electing such individuals—we are responsible for our leaders.

The impact on our lives can be great from doing evil. We know from the Bible that there is not always a direct relationship between sin and immediate punishment. Solomon, the wisest man who ever lived, said that "time and chance happen to every man." Jesus stated that those who were sacrificed and those on whom the tower fell in Siloam were not guiltier than all others. Yet Jesus also told one of the paralyzed men he healed to "stop sinning or something worse may happen to you."

Thus, there is not always a direct relationship between sin and immediate punishment. But this is largely because of God's mercy. When we do evil, we may or may not be punished, but have no illusion—if we are not punished, this does mean that we got away with the evil. I believe that God looks at the pattern of our behavior to determine whether or not we are committed to his son Jesus Christ (and hence, to him) or if we are simply claiming to be a follower of God. Those who claim to believe in God but reject all or part of his word in favor of their preferred lifestyle or their own beliefs will likely be judged as hypocrites. They may claim that they follow God, but God knows whether they have submitted to his commands. People in this country say they follow God, yet in the same breath they support abortion or homosexual activities. This cannot be so if they truly follow God.

Strangely, one of the most merciful things that God can do for us is to punish us when we sin. Why? Because if we are somewhat introspective, we may consider that the punishment we receive signifies a need to repent—to turn away from—a given sin or lifestyle, and that means, then, that the punishment has served its purpose—it has refocused us back on God. Punishment is just one of the ways that God gets our attention. Like the gambling addict or the drug dealer, however, who must lose everything before he is able to turn his life around, we in this county risk losing everything because of our steadfast will to refuse the Lord's commands. We would be much better off to obey now than to lose everything because we refuse to repent.

Man thinks that he has the right to evaluate God by his own set of values and limited intelligence. Many people believe themselves to be master of all they survey. Yet this is a trap directly from the evil one. Why? It is because the devil directly influences man by building up man's pride, so that he believes himself to either be equal to God—and thus can judge him—or superior to God, obviating the need for God and his commands. Yet you would be surprised how many people turn to God when the going gets rough. Pride is the same sin for which the devil was punished.

The God of the Bible has put before each of us a choice, and he has granted us a free will to choose for ourselves: the God of the Bible and his son, or against God and his son. Choosing him and his son leads to salvation; all others choices lead to destruction. There are other religions but no other gods. It is our choice to choose life or to choose death, but make no mistake—God will allow us to make this choice, knowing that the only true choice exists when a choice is made within the framework of free will.

The choice is for each one of us individually and for this country. We will choose for the God of the Bible and seek to obey him completely, or we will choose some other path. This life means little in the greater scheme of things, primarily because it represents an infinitesimally small fraction of the time that we exist. You and I will exist forever. Our choice will determine how we spend that time.

Listen to the words of the Lord in Jeremiah 18:7–12: *If at any time I announce that a nation or kingdom is to be uprooted, torn down and destroyed, and if that nation I warned repents of its evil, then I will relent and not inflict on it the disaster I had planned. And if at another time I announce that a nation or kingdom is to be built up and planted, and if it does evil in my sight and does not obey me, then I will reconsider the good I had intended to do for it. "Now therefore say to the people of Judah and those living in Jerusalem, this is what the LORD says: Look! I am preparing a disaster for you and devising a plan against you. So turn from your evil ways, each one of you, and reform your ways and your actions." But they will reply, "It's no use. We will continue with our own plans; each of us will follow the stubbornness of his evil heart."*

God is directly involved in which nations prosper and which nations suffer. In an environment where we are allowed to exist with a free will, the majority of people will gravitate toward their own sinful desires, but we must resist those desires and refocus this country on following God's commands. These also are warnings to our nation, which started out following God, but which has slowly but surely wandered away from our God. I fear for what will happen to this nation if we do not return to God and forsake our abominable practices.

This country *was* great because the people who founded it agreed on a common set of values (God's values). God blessed this country because of this; indeed, we have been the most blessed nation on earth, but like the country of Israel's historical rebellion, we have ignored what God says about remaining pure and devoted to him. We have done this by adopting many of the practices of our country's immigrants. It is not that people from other countries are not welcome; rather, it is that we must be strong enough to maintain our godly laws in this country, regardless of what our country's immigrants want to do.

This is not about any type of hate; it is about doing what is right. There is a very simple connection between forsaking the Lord and our country's future; it goes something like this: We forsake the Lord's laws, and he forsakes us as a country. We adhere to his laws, and he blesses this country. We can continue to push the Lord out of our lives, but guess what? If we are unwilling to acknowledge his ways as right, we should not expect the Lord to answer us when we get into trouble. I promise you that no amount of military force can protect us without God's blessing. Conversely, if we submit to God and his commands, even if we are not at the top of our game, militarily, God can protect us. Will we trust in God, or will we trust in our own abilities?

RIGHT AND WRONG

What is right? What is wrong? Ask these questions to ten different people and you are likely to get ten different answers. This underscores the basic problem with human-centered morality; there is no standard among humans for what is right or wrong. Think about this: Are there humans on this earth who believe that adultery is okay? Are there humans on this earth who believe that stealing is okay? Are there humans on this earth who believe that murder is okay? In *all* cases, the answer is yes. This, as much as anything, gets us into trouble. In addition, we have a sinful nature, and so our tendency is to continue to shift our morality toward more evil and depraved practices. There is a standard for right and wrong, and we must not only acknowledge it, but we also must seek to live by it.

The commands of God are a blessing. Just as we get older and become thankful for our parents' guidance when we were children, so we should be thankful for God's guidance, as he knows more than we do. Look at all of the problems that have occurred in this world because leaders or the people they led did not use the Bible as their standard of right and wrong. Hitler, Hussein, Pol Pot, Idi Amin, Stalin—the list could go on and on, depending on how far back in history you want to go. As a side note, some of the most atrocious acts in history have been justified in the name of religion, but *claiming* to be a Christian does not make you a Christian, any more than walking into a garage makes you a car. God knows whether you are reading his word, seeking his will, and trying to obey him.

Too many of us in this country have given up trying to do right and have given in to our selfish desires or have ignored the wrong that others do. We have come under the influence of those who refuse to acknowledge the only valid standard for right and wrong. The very soul and future of our country, not to mention the future for us as individuals, is at stake because of this. We must get back to doing what is right, forsaking what is wrong. If those who do not want to follow God's commands do not want to live here, that is fine; they are welcome to leave, but we must not let them hijack the morals of this country, which should be based on God's commands.

Who influences us? In this country, organizations like the American Civil Liberties Union (ACLU), media outlets, and celebrities are examples of sources of influence, and they are dangerous. Why? It is because they set themselves up against the wisdom, morals, and values of God, leading others to oppose God as well. Popular celebrities, for example, support both abortion and homosexuality, both of which God has forbidden. Are we more willing to listen to famous people on this earth than to the God who created us? Many people who assume that because these famous people have been so blessed, they must be right. Nothing could be farther from the truth. Some of the greatest people in the Bible had nothing, but they were distinguished from those who opposed God by their ability to tell right from wrong, using God's standard. Obeying God was the basis for God's approval in biblical times, and it still is today. Wealth and riches mean absolutely zero if you don't have God's values supporting them, for as Christ said "what good is it for a man to gain the whole world, yet forfeit his soul?"

People who listen to organizations, media outlets, or celebrities often follow them and adopt their positions on issues, as if that were a recipe for success. In some cases, these entities deliberately mislead us; in other cases, they are simply deceived. They have becomes masters of substituting half-truths for the actual truth, and they do not tell the whole story. They substitute their own truths for the real truth. They hide things that they don't want people to know and promote to front pages the things they want to promote—in short, they try to manipulate us. Unfortunately, the attempt at manipulation is leading us away from God, not toward him.

There are even more extreme elements in our society. There is the Rational Response Squad (which I feel should be called the "Irrational" Response Squad), a group of atheists that advocates blasphemy against God and the Holy Spirit and entices others to rebel against God. They assume the most arrogant of stances, claiming there is no God. Like those suffering from the Stockholm syndrome, who have been mentally captured as hostages by the devil, these individuals are so tightly under Satan's control that they are doing his work for him without even realizing they are under his control. They have lost their free will. They have lost the ability to recognize truth and have seared their consciences. They are the "brute beasts" written about almost two thousand years ago, and like the beasts, they will be caught and destroyed. We can only pray they come to their senses before it is too late.

People who get caught up in the activities and posturing of such entities and who don't have an authoritative standard by which to judge right from wrong, often end up under the influence of such ungodly entities. As such, they become unaware participants in opposing God. We have allowed freedom of speech to become a negative in this country, as it is used to advocate all forms of evil, even though the evil is often camouflaged as protection of First Amendment rights. But just like yelling "fire" in a crowded theatre, such expressions of freedom are being misused to mislead people into devastation.

We have *no* right to do evil, and we will suffer if we insist on doing evil—period! Our reckoning day is coming, and the only way to avoid it is to return to the Lord and accept his ways as ours. We can ignore the Lord, we can oppose the Lord, and we can refuse to believe in the Lord, but it will not change the outcome of what our choice brings us. (Similarly, ignoring, opposing, or refusing to believing in gravity is dangerous as well, as doing so will not change out outcome either.) We are all under the authority of Jesus, who sacrificed himself for all of us, but just like gravity, which we cannot see, if we ignore or refuse that authority, we will pay for refusing that authority.

Individuals or entities who espouse such extreme and unfounded positions are easier to identify. With regard to those leading or seeking to lead this country, the challenge becomes much more complex. Some leaders are trying to do right, but their actions betray them, showing they have been deceived. It is stunning to see how many people refuse to seek the entire counsel of God utilizing selective verses without the proper context. Some of them cannot identify right from wrong because they simply refuse to use God's standard of right and wrong. Still others know what their responsibilities are, but they refuse to take those responsibilities seriously and prefer to seek their own good rather than the good of this country.

Enter our responsibilities in this matter ...

As individuals, we must be careful who we support and who we vote into office. When we vote for individuals who do not have values and morals consistent with what God commands, we are just as guilty of sin as they are, because we have voted to have someone represent our views and morals. This is the nature of a representative government. This is a government by the people for the people. Their sin becomes our sin. We can claim that we have no control over what the elected person does, but in most cases, this is no more than passing the buck. Most politicians are brazen enough to state ungodly positions, and yet we still vote for them. Hence, when we vote for those who refuse to submit to God's commands, we are in effect rejecting God.

The essence of this is important: for the upcoming 2008 election, candidates have espoused all sorts of religious affiliations. Religion is not the issue; the issue is the ability to make moral decisions, based on a non-relative standard of right and wrong. Those who claim to follow God through their words but still insist on advocating abortion, for example, show their true character; they cannot be truly seeking God. If they cared about God, they would learn what he seeks. If they cannot make the choice on such a basic issue and align themselves with God, how can we trust them to make good decisions on other important issues?

If they start out espousing godly positions (e.g., consistent with biblical teachings) and then vote or change their positions and adopt ungodly practices, we must be prepared to recall them. We simply cannot be apathetic about this any longer; we need to get involved and stop our leaders from acting in an ungodly manner. What does God say about this? Here the words of God from Jeremiah 6:18–19: *Therefore hear, O nations; observe, O witnesses, what will happen to them. Hear, O earth: I am bringing disaster on this people, the fruit of their schemes, because they have not listened to my words and have rejected my law.*

Although these words were spoken against Israel, they apply to us as well. Let's make sure we understand the subtleties of this sin. We should be under no illusion—we all (and I do mean all) sin against the Lord. What separates those who submit to God and those who don't submit to God is their attitude toward sin. A person who submits to God uses God's definition of right and wrong, adopting that standard as his or her own, attempting to avoid sin and trying to do what is right, based on God's word. He or she takes positions on issues consistent with God's teachings and supports those who are committed to the same teachings. It is not that Christians don't sin—they absolutely do—but they do try to avoid sin, and they accept God's commands as they are.

Those who will not submit to God live in rebellion against God. They believe they have the right to change God's rules or interpret God's rules as they see fit, believing in human self-direction and effectively ignoring God. They take positions on issues that are clearly opposed to God's laws, and they have no problem trying to entice the electorate to support them in their positions. They will be revealed as hypocrites when the Lord returns. This is the basis of the Lord's claim that he would say "I never knew you." Hence, these people lead our country away from God, not closer to God.

We can think of all kinds of rationalization for voting the way we do and supporting the individuals we do, but if we, as voters, elect individuals who oppose God's teachings, we are a party to their evil, and we are guilty of sin, because essentially, we are saying that we approve of what they do. Enough! We need to stand up for what is right according to the Lord's standards. If we do not have the courage and integrity to do what is right, then we will pay with our very blood.

We cannot claim to follow someone if we don't accept what he teaches. Anyone who claims to follow Christ but does not do what he says is a hypocrite, and Christ has warned what will happen to hypocrites. Of course, there are also debatable issues; I acknowledge this, as do most others. This book is not designed to address every conceivable issue, but we must at least get the basics right. If we have the basics right, most times we will address debatable issues correctly. If, however, we do not even have the basics right, we will flounder on the more debatable issues.

Let me touch upon a subject that is near and dear to most of the American public: the Iraq War. Pursuing the Iraq War is a good example of a debatable issue, although much of this county feels that the war was and is wrong. Personally, I am not able to distinguish the true motives behind the war. I will acknowledge that the United States initially went to war based on faulty information. Whether the information was intentionally falsely reported is not the issue here, and we may never authoritatively know this. We may quarrel with the basis of the why, but let's take an objective look at what has happened.

Our American heroes are sacrificing their lives so that others can live in freedom. In some parts of Iraq, this freedom has been realized. Many have died, but the toll is much less than in our own bloody wars for freedom (Revolutionary, Civil). Our heroes have given their lives to save their brothers and sisters in Iraq, to save children from violence and death and from chaos. Does it come at a high price? Yes, it does, but I have utmost respect for those who give their lives for their brothers and sisters in Iraq (we are all brothers and sisters). Yet there are vast segments of the public as well as politicians who are angry that we are still in Iraq and who actually want us to lose the war. Most of these individuals have no godly basis for their anger; rather, they are selfish because they are ashamed of our military forces—armed by people who love others enough to sacrifice their lives, even as many others live a life of self-indulgence. The example that our military sets shames them.

I can certainly empathize—but only at a surface level—with those who have lost children or other loved ones in the war. This is a terrible tragedy, but they have done one thing that most of us have not. They have given their lives to protect the innocent and to give one of the most precious gifts to their brothers and sisters in Iraq: freedom. We who sit back and criticize them have not been willing to sacrifice ourselves for others, and many of us are envious because they have been willing to make the sacrifices that we, in selfishness, have not. Rather, too many of us are so selfish and self-absorbed that we have lost touch with the purer virtues. They are helping others and are paying with the most valuable thing they have: their lives. Here, we sit in judgment of our heroes, even to the level of wanting them to fail. That is pure hatred—hatred for those who sacrifice their lives to try to help others. What is the matter with us?

Let's ask ourselves what is causing us to be upset. Are we upset that our heroes are giving their lives for their Iraqi brothers and sisters? Are we upset that our heroes are protecting the lives of innocent children and the Iraqis by trying to do what is right? Are we upset that our heroes want to give the gift of freedom to the people of Iraq after suffering through years of genocide and domination? The reason that many of us hate this war is because we have lost touch with the noblest of motives that many of our American heroes are pursuing. We are so very selfish that we sit in judgment of our heroes, using our warped sense of morality.

Some members of the military want nothing to do with this war, and some members of the military and civilian forces alike have acted inappropriately, but neither of these are reasons to abandon the good that has been brought to the Iraqi people. Are people dying there? Of course! Are they suffering? Of course! But remember that we Americans fought a war for independence so that we might have freedom, and many lives were lost and many suffered. Now, because we have lost the ability to identify with the goal of freedom, we think the suffering of the Iraqi people is crazy. We also cannot identify with those who were persecuted in Iraq under Saddam Hussein. Some in this country had the courage to stand on their convictions and Iraq is now showing signs of great improvement. What would have happened to our consciences in this country if we had heeded the calls of some to pullout at any cost, leaving the Iraqi people to the terrorists who wanted to destroy their country? Sometimes doing what is right has costs, but the cost of refusing to do right, of being selfish, is our souls. This is what the war is about in this country today.

The war does cost money, the war does cost lives, and the war has hurt this country. If we were to look back, perhaps we would determine that we should not have started this war, but even so, I would counsel caution. Right now, it is the selfishness of some people within this country that demands that we abandon the Iraqi people, leaving them to the mercies of aggressive terrorists within their society. Suppose terrorists started attacking individuals in the United States (which is likely forthcoming). We would *beg* our military to protect us. This is what we are doing for those in Iraq.

For what it is worth, I want the U.S. to get out of Iraq as well, but I do not want the U.S. to pull out at any cost, which is what many advocate. Societies have to undertake sacrifices from time to time. Our military understands this, but our politicians and too many of our citizens do not. While we can debate whether we should have ever gone into Iraq, we are there now, and it is irresponsible to simply evacuate the country, leaving the Iraqi people to the killers in their society. I still believe that the Iraqi people are better off now, and many of us forget how many lives were lost in our own country for our independence. We were liberated from another country's control, but Iraqi's have been liberated from a dictator who was, in effect, committing genocide.

Why are the American public and American politicians trying to make this into a bad thing? Once again, we are not applying God's values but our own. Our heroes understand what they are doing; they see the faces of the children they are helping, the people they are protecting, and the freedom that is being bestowed. They understand we fought a war for freedom, which cost many lives, but too many people have forgotten what we are about. This is why we should be supporting our troops—because they are doing great things for others and giving of themselves, while we sit at home and selfishly whine about them. Shame on us!

The Bible says that authorities bear the sword for a reason, and only God knows our true motive for being in Iraq. If it really is to grant freedom to our Iraqi brothers, then it is the noblest of callings and the greatest show of love for those we love to sacrifice themselves for others. If the true motive for the Iraq War is to secure access to oil for this country over the long term or some other selfish motive, then it is the wrong motive. God knows the truth, but rest assured, he understands the sacrifice of our heroes as they lay down their lives for their Iraqi brothers and sisters. Those who espouse contempt for our military have lost contact with what freedom means and don't understand the price that we paid for our own freedom. God help us if we ever have to defend our freedom again. I fear that most who oppose the war will likely abandon this country in its hour of need. In reality, our country ought to be involved everywhere that a cruel and despicable leader commits atrocities against the people. That is a failing of the United States today.

But this is only one area in which we are struggling because we cannot appreciate godly values. Let's look at the more basic tenets that God teaches and see how we, as a country, have substituted the truth of God with human teachings. See if you can identify the types of evil that these perceptions have fostered (every one of these leads to practices that violate the commands of God):

- Life doesn't begin until birth.

- Suicide is okay if you are in great pain.

- We must separate church and state.

- The luxuries we lavish on our animals are more important than preventing poor children from dying every day.

- It is offensive to others to pray or recite the Bible.

- Sex outside of marriage is okay if you love someone.

- You have to be who you are.

- Getting drunk is okay so long as you don't drive.

- Homosexuality is genetic.

- Lying is okay.

- Any religion is okay, regardless of what it teaches, as long as it's peaceful.

- God is so loving that he would never consign anyone to hell.

- If you live a "good" life, you will be with God.

- You have earned everything you have, so it is yours.

While these points are scary enough, can you imagine what other evils we can come up with in the future as we travel down the road of relative truth? Consider, for a moment, that there is *no* evil that cannot be justified through some relative truth. I can invent reasons for virtually any type of evil, and this is where we are heading. Relative truth is probably the single greatest failing of the human race. People will say that what is true to them is not necessarily true for others. More often than not there are absolutes for right and wrong for most actions but we have substituted feelings for basic truths. We have become so good at this we now treat abortion, which is essentially murder into something which is justified through people's feelings. There is an absolute standard for what is right and what is wrong. That standard is God and his word (the Bible), but we must be able to accept it as it is.

I know that some are skeptical that the Bible is the word of God, preferring to view it as a collection of stories written by men. Those who are willing to look objectively at the origins of the works, however— comparing archaeological history with biblical claims, seeing that secular works provide referential evidence, and noting the timing of certain writings (prophecies) contrasted with later occurrences—will generally conclude that the preponderance of evidence suggests that the Bible is, in fact, accurate.

In the United States we have what is called the "burden of proof." The burden of proof is also called the balance of probabilities, which is generally ascribed to be more than 50 percent, or tipping the balance of the scales in one towards one side or the other since a scale will tip one way or the other as soon as one side contains more than 50% of the total weight . We also have "beyond a reasonable doubt," which means highly likely but without an objective measure. These two terms have been presented here because they are relevant to belief in the Bible as the word of God.

The Bible is "beyond a reasonable doubt" the word of God—the evidence suggests that it is highly likely that the Bible is the word of God. Consider the following inescapable facts surrounding the Bible.

- The Bible was written over the course of many years, by many authors, and in multiple languages, yet is cohesive in both its purpose and message.

- The Bible has been shown to be historically accurate, more so than any other historical book, with more original copies and cross-references available than any other historical book.

- The Bible contains specific prophecies dated to a given period, which occurred later, exactly as predicted. Many of these prophecies are specific. This in itself is a supernatural signature that cannot be dismissed, except by those who are irrational in their attempts to discredit the Bible.

- Jesus was a real person, referenced by both Jewish and secular scholars, and accredited with miraculous works, even by those who opposed the Jews and their religion.

- Apostles selected by Jesus were fearful and fled before he was crucified, but after having witnessed his resurrection, they gladly gave their lives for him. They were martyred for their faith, demonstrating a change of character based on facts. Surely if they had been convinced that Jesus was a fake, they would not have given their lives and would have found some way to avoid being martyred.

Thus, the Bible is the word of God beyond reasonable doubt. I am sure there are many who will not accept this, yet I would ask you to consider that those who will not accept the Bible as accurate will accept concepts with far less evidence supporting them. Here are a few questions that those who oppose the Bible have no trouble overlooking:

- What caused the Big Bang?

- What did the universe consist of before the Big Bang?

- Where are the full set of types and populations of intermediate forms espoused in Darwin's theory?

- Where do people get their consciences?

- What are the mathematical chances of life forming exactly in this manner, given all of the requirements?

The fundamental issue is this: men and women who do not believe in God believe they are God. They may not say so directly, but they believe it indirectly, because they believe they can use their limited intellects (and we all have limited intellects, compared to a being that can create the universe) to reason that there is no God, even though there are far too many things they cannot explain. They, as beings with limited intellects, assess a given set of events and then say to themselves that because things did not turn out the way that they expected, God doesn't exist. It is fallacious activity for a being with a limited intellect and limited knowledge to judge a being with unlimited intellect and unlimited knowledge. Once a person starts down this path, however, he sets his own reality, his own morals, and his own truths, and from this we get into a big problem: relative truth.

In this world, relative truth is referred to as diversity. Many counsel us to tolerate others and their views in the name of diversity, allowing them to develop or perceive their own truth by not criticizing what they believe. Unfortunately, this is, by definition, chaos. While we generally use human law as the basis of what is acceptable and what is not acceptable, the law continues to change, to embody more questionable practices, and to allow more things that are evil. At the same time, it distances itself from the commands of God. Technically, we have no right to condemn suicide bombers because we must acknowledge that they are doing what they believe is right. If we reject God's standard of truth for our own truth, how can we then reject someone else's version of the truth?

Here is an extreme example, but I believe this example will make the point: God condemns homosexuality. Those who practice homosexuality believe it is okay. Those in Iran believe it is okay to torture and kill homosexuals. Who is right here? It is pure hypocrisy for a person who practices homosexuality to say his views on homosexuality are right but then to deny others the same right to their own view, even if their view is that those who practice homosexuality are worthy of death. Why? Because neither of these (practicing homosexuality or killing those who practice homosexuality) are right, based on God's standard, an absolute standard. Both are right, however, if you allow an individual to set the standard of right and wrong.

Furthermore, people have not taken the time to truly understand the word of God. This should be one of the most important things they can do—understanding the desires of their Creator. By not investing the time to understand what God commands, the Bible causes people to act and espouse incorrect positions. As a simple example, God commands us through his word not to kill. The underlying Hebrew word ratsach (רצח), however, really means murder. Killing and murdering can be vastly different things, based on the circumstances, yet people will misuse the text to mean that all killing is wrong. This alone can cause people to not want to follow God, because they believe they cannot protect themselves or their family or that this country cannot protect itself if it involves killing.

The same misunderstanding exists about the government. Many think that the government should act the same as we individuals are called to do which is not necessarily true. The government should not in any way be corrupt but the Bible recognizes that governments do "bear the sword" for a reason and we must acknowledge this.

What many people have trouble with is setting their own morality. There is an absolute truth about many issues, but we must be able to accept it. Individuals who want to set their own morals fall into a trap, in that they are unwilling to allow others to do the same thing. They say that they think it is okay to commit adultery or have an abortion, but they then decry as wrong those people who say that they think it is okay to kill others. That is hypocrisy! You cannot reserve for yourself the right to set your own morals and deny others the same right, regardless of how heinous you believe those morals to be. Thus, we need to rely on an absolute truth, where there is one available, and God's teachings fill that role.

In a democracy there are plenty of areas in which laws need to be established and enforced, and for some of these there are no specific godly teachings. But let's not make the mistake of making laws that are inconsistent with God's laws. Where God speaks, we should listen; where God is silent, we can speak. For example, if we, as a nation, were to pass a law that states that anyone older than sixty should be euthanized, we would be passing a law that legitimizes murder. If we pass a law that says abortion is legal, we are passing a law that legitimizes murder. We can insist that it is not murder because those over sixty take more from society than they give, or that an unborn human being is not really alive, but these are fallacious arguments. Murder is murder—period! We can sugar-coat it, re-title it, or try to justify it, but it is still legalized murder and is in conflict with what God teaches.

Those who would argue that the voice of the people rules in a democracy are attempting to justify evil because many people believe in it. This is another fallacious line of thought. Our laws must not oppose our Creator's laws, or we will feel his wrath. How many times throughout history have large groups of people paid the price because they did not know right from wrong? We must be strong in this democracy to hold to God's commands, first and foremost, and not let those who are committed to opposing God sway us into the same rebellion or engender enough apathy in us to cause us to sit by and watch as they destroy this country.

How does this happen? It is because people do not agree on a standard by which to judge whether a law is morally right, and because people, when left to their own devices, lean toward evil. (Romans 7:18: *I know that nothing good lives in me; that is, in my sinful nature. For I have the desire to do what is good, but I cannot carry it out.*) I know this because I see it in myself and at times struggle with my sinful nature. The reason that the United States has existed as long as it has and that we have been so blessed is that the initial basis of our government acknowledged God as the definitive source of what is right and what is wrong.

Although we have many self-professed Christians in this country, how many of them can say they have read God's word cover to cover even once? How can those who claim to be Christian know if they are submitting to the demands of their God if they won't even take the time to read his word? If all of the self-proclaimed Christians actually read the word of God, we would have much less support for ungodly practices, such as abortion. We would also have a much less apathetic populace, as they would have a solid grasp of where this country is heading. They would get involved if for no other reason than to help those know God and to know what he wants.

As we move farther and farther away from God and his values, supplanting God's influence in our government with human-centric values and ideals, the blessings that this country has enjoyed will continue to disappear, and we will suffer greatly! It has already begun.

As the 2008 presidential primary season unfolded, much of the American public seemed to caucus toward a change in leadership, but the answer is not a less godly leader. Yes, it is true that many leaders have done unconscionable things to the American public in the past, but the answer is not to vote for a leader who advocates ungodly positions. Doing so will lead each of us and this country into countless troubles. My fellow countrymen and countrywomen, please compare your preferred candidates' views with the commands of God, and support, first and foremost, those who advocate following God's commands. Look carefully at the potential candidates and see what they are doing.

Currently, some presidential candidates have met with those who espouse hate, publish pornography, and engage in every form of sin. The presidential candidates fear them and are more interested in votes at any cost than in doing what is right. This alone should disqualify them from leading a country. How can this country stand if we elect leaders without the courage to stand up to evil? We cannot! Other presidential candidates are willing to unconditionally meet with any world leaders, even if those leaders are calling for genocide of a people. How can this country stand if we elect leaders with no commitment to doing what is right? We cannot! My fellow countrymen, if we vote for those leaders who have no moral integrity and who follow relative truth as their standard of right and wrong, we will get a government with *no* moral integrity, and it is we who will suffer. God will punish us if we do not care enough to seek to elect those who will do what is right.

Also, we need to be careful about moving toward a one-world government, which is simply another way to introduce a series of ungodly practices into this country by other populations that have traditionally not followed God. If the choice is a one-world government with ungodly practices and peace, or a multi-world government that follows God's laws with constant strife, we are better off with the latter. All obstacles can be surmounted with God. Surmounting even the most basic obstacles is difficult without him. We must remain true to our God and must return to obeying his commands, regardless of what other countries of the world do. If we do not have the courage to submit to our God and do what he commands, our destruction will be on our own heads.

We can argue about the reason for all of this country's problems, but it truly all boils down to one fundamental issue: we are unwilling to acknowledge God's commands, to make laws consistent with his commands, and to live by his commands, even though this has worked for more than two hundred years. We think that we know more than God and can make our own laws, but I challenge you to study God's commands (not just the Ten Commandments but all of his commands), and then ask yourself: what problems would we have if we simply followed his commands?

If we vote to elect a person because he or she is black or because he or she is white but has the wrong morals, we are at fault. If we vote to elect a person because he or she is Southern but has the wrong morals, we are at fault. If we vote for a person because he or she is a Republican but has the wrong morals, we are at fault. If we vote for a person because she is female but has the wrong morals, we are at fault. We must subject every candidate to the "truth" test. If that candidate cannot acknowledge the only true standard for right and wrong—and follow it—we should not be voting for that person.

This country does not have to be organized as a religious theocracy to be blessed by God. Indeed, we have traditionally been blessed because our laws were based on God's laws and because we have acknowledged God. So while a democratic government works fine, we must have laws that mirror God's laws if we expect to merit his blessings and avoid his wrath. We must remain true to our God. We cannot be carried away to follow all sorts of other gods (there is only one true God), other religions, ungodly practices, or unjust laws, even if the majority of the country wants them. We must utilize God's word and God's word alone as the foundation for our laws.

Entire organizations may believe they are doing what is right in trying to separate church and state, but all they are doing is convincing others to turn their backs on God, which will result in the destruction of this nation. Whether they realize it or not, they are under Satan's influence and are doing the will of their master by stripping the moral backbone from this nation. Due to these organizations which are committed to trying to separate church and state, this county is facing its most severe challenges ever, and they are about to get worse—not worse because we are in Iraq or are challenging Iran but worse because we are losing our moral compass. The more influence we let these organizations have over us and the more we follow their immoral counsel, the more damage they will do to this country and its people. We can only pray that they also come to their senses and support the God who loves them, rather than the evil one, who in the end, will destroy them.

The United States has always allowed individuals from other countries to come to this land, and they have traditionally been a blessing to this country. But our laws have remained our laws, our language remained our language, and our morals remained our morals. Now our laws, our language, and our morals are under attack to protect ungodly and evil practices. We who call ourselves followers of God seem to be unwilling to stand up for what is right, often being carried along with others. Just as the Israelites of old adopted the ungodly practices of the nations around them, so we are doing the same thing.

Let's be clear: We cannot use a "truth" based on the Koran, based on the Book of Mormon, based on the Bhagavad Gita, or based any document except the Bible. Does this sound intolerant? It probably does, but then again, the truth always has been intolerant because it deals in fewer shades of gray than people are comfortable with. Yet people's tolerance can change over time, and left to their own desires, they are capable of unspeakable evil if they do not have an absolute standard for right and wrong.

Fifty years ago, adultery was not tolerated; now it is a common practice. Fifty years ago, it would have been unthinkable for people to go out in public without wearing underwear; now it is common. Fifty years ago, molesting children was the most heinous of crimes; now it is not only common but some judges refuse to sentence convicted offenders, which denies justice to the most innocent of victims. We aren't enlightened; we are drowning in evil. Look for a person who spends his time trying to find extreme examples of where a truth breaks down, and you'll find a person who is not committed to truth. There are gray issues, but there are also black-and-white issues.

My fellow countrymen and countrywomen let us return to God, the only true author of morality.

GET THE HYPOCRISY OUT!

What is a hypocrite? A hypocrite is an individual who claims one thing and then acts in a manner inconsistent with those claims. Merriam-Webster defines a hypocrite as "a person who puts on a false appearance of virtue or religion" or "a person who acts in contradiction to his or her stated beliefs or feelings."

This happens to be a failing of many people who claim to follow God. They claim to follow God and then act in a manner inconsistent with what they claim. Now, before your feathers are ruffled, understand that we all fail God; none of us is perfect. Here is the subtlety, however, that many people miss. There is a difference between those who oppose the teaching of God on one or more points and those who submit to all of God's teaching but sin at various points. You either accept all of what God teaches, or you are living in rebellion to him.

If you claim that you believe you can fly, I expect to see you jumping off tall buildings and flying. Otherwise, I will assume you are a hypocrite (i.e., that you don't really believe that you can fly). The same is true with almost anything else. If you really believe the stock market is going up, I expect you to invest most of your money there. If you do not, I will conclude you don't really believe what you are saying. The same is true with Christ. If you claim you believe in him, your actions must generally mirror Christ's teachings and actions; otherwise, you do not really believe and are a hypocrite. Too many of our leaders act hypocritically, claiming to follow God, primarily for the sake of acquiring support, but then acting in rebellion to God and leading this country into destruction. They go to church—and then support the

29

killing of babies. They read the Bible—and then have no problem with adulterous relationships. They claim to follow Christ—and then see no problem with pornography.

If you oppose God on even one of his commands, you have assumed a prideful position that tells God that you know more than he does—and that is just arrogance, the very sin of Satan. God is God; we are his children. Just as we, as parents, know more than our children, so does God know more than we do. If we oppose God's teachings, even on one point, we are guilty of the same sin of which Satan is guilty—pride. Once you start down that path, it is only a matter of time before you start questioning other commands of God. Such people are not fit to be leaders. Look at what happened to Israel when evil kings reigned.

But more important than this is the fact that we support politicians who reject God—or worse, claim to follow God but do not do what he says. Our fate will be the same as those politicians who claim to know God but do not obey him. If we support ungodly leaders, we are opposing God and he may simply not be there for us when we get in trouble. This is because we have rejected him based on the fact that we were hypocritical in saying that we followed Jesus and then turned around and voted for leaders who are committed to violating his commands. If we tell someone else it's okay to steal, even though we don't, we are responsible. If we vote for someone who supports abortion, even though we don't have an abortion, we are responsible. Furthermore, just as the Israelites who supported ungodly kings paid the price, so this country will pay a similar price. Impossible, you say? I assure you it is not.

If we want God's blessings on our country and want to avoid the penalties for violating his commands, we need to follow his commands. How does this translate? It translates to outlawing abortion; outlawing homosexuality and same-sex marriages; discouraging sexual liaisons outside of marriage; allowing worship of God in public places, regardless of who is offended by it; and many other similar laws. Does this seem too radical for you? Would you consider it radical if you knew that failing to do these things would result in certain death? Some may claim "Live free or die." We are free, but we are not free to do evil. The very people who would claim "Live free or die" operate under this philosophy—as long as no one else uses their freedom to hurt them!

The laws that make ungodly activities legal must be repealed if we are to escape God's wrath.

We cannot grow tired of doing what is right. Recently, a school district in Portland, ME (King Middle School) started handing out birth control to eleven-year-old girls without parental consent. Why? Because parents are no longer willing to dictate a hard line of what is right and wrong. From the school's perspective, they don't want to expend the effort to deal with the root cause of the problem, so they try to address a subsequent symptom. I am sure it is only a matter of time before we legalize drug use, spousal abuse, honor killing, and some additional forms of murder. Before you say that could never happen, drug use is already starting to become more common. Marijuana use was recently legalized in Denver even though it violates federal law. Spousal abuse is legal in some places; in fact, so is rape. (Recently, a rape victim in another country was sentenced to two hundred lashes.) Honor killings occur routinely around the globe and are suspected to have occurred recently here in the United states. Murder? Maybe it will take longer, but I am sure there will come a point when we will need to sacrifice weaker individuals so that the stronger will flourish, or we'll sacrifice those whose morals do not match the morals of our country.

I know that the temptation must be great to believe that because God has not punished or destroyed us, he is okay with what we are doing. Do not misconstrue the great mercy of God with apathy or indifference. He has given us much time to repent, to follow him, but just like the examples in the Bible, when God decides to act, he will act with swiftness and finality, and there will be nowhere else to turn when our God is angry. Who will save us from his wrath?

We love our children. Some of us love them enough to even give our lives for them, but we will not tolerate all actions they perform, just because we love them. Although God's mercy is much, much greater than ours, there will come a time when he says enough and will punish us for our actions. Please, my fellow citizens, do not delay in returning to God and his values.

Now, to those who do not know Jesus Christ and claim that "Christians" are sinners as well, we Christians acknowledge their correctness. Many will claim that self-proclaimed Christians are hypocrites. This could be the case! Only the Lord knows for sure who is and who is not a hypocrite. If self-proclaimed Christians sin, that does not make them hypocrites, although they should certainly try to avoid sinning. Self-proclaimed Christians are hypocrites if they oppose what God teaches. Just because people sin does not, in itself, make them a hypocrite.

There is a profound difference between those who reject the teachings of God and continue to sin, and those who seek to avoid sin and repent when they do sin. Even in man's justice system there is likely to be more mercy for the convicted criminal who demonstrates contrition before a judge than the one who is disdainful of the law under which he has been convicted.

Those who are Christians should try to obey God's laws so as to please God but also so that they are witnesses for the nonbelievers. Nonbelievers take note, though, in this example: if I exceed the speed limit when I drive, but I counsel you not to speed when you are driving, it may make me a hypocrite but it does not invalidate the advice. This is why we are all called to follow Jesus, the one who taught us, having established himself as the standard of perfection. Right is right and wrong is wrong, regardless of who is offering the counsel—as long as it is based on the standard of truth. Consider for yourself that judges often break the law, but that does not render them incapable of performing their judicial duties.

All people fit into one of three groups. The first group is composed of individuals who accept God's word and try to live according to it. Although they stumble from time to time, they repent, seek God's forgiveness, and try to get back to living according to God's laws. They make a conscious effort to avoid breaking God's commands. God speaks of these people as worshipping in spirit and truth. Their actions confirm their beliefs.

The second group acknowledges the God of the Bible but does not live according to what God teaches. They either do not love God enough to seek to fully understand his commands or, in some cases, they choose to accept only part of God's commands. For those commands that they do not wish to follow, they simply ignore God's commands or replace God's commands with their own teachings. This shows up in the decisions they make, the individuals they support, and the positions they take on important issues. These are people who claim to love God but live in rebellion to him. This is the group I hope to reach with this book. If you are one of these people, I implore you to seek the

God of the Bible on his terms and make decisions in your life that are consistent with what he commands. If you do not, how can you escape the scathing words of the Lord—"I never knew you!"— on the day that you face him?

We need to be careful with regard to where we get our teachings from God. We are *all* responsible for what is in the Bible. We will not be able to say that the pastor said this or the evangelist said that as an excuse for why we did not follow God's word. Many leading churches today are led by individuals who are out for personal gain, individuals who are leading by using hollow, human philosophies that conflict with the word of God. These individuals are not willing to submit to God. The condemnation that these people receive is hanging over their heads. We can only pray they repent before it is too late.

The third group does not acknowledge the God of the Bible or his son Jesus Christ or their authority over their lives. We pray that these people will come to know the mercy of the Lord and the truth and that they will recognize the sacrifice undertaken by Jesus because he loves us. There are many false religions in the world. I would ask you to seriously look at what has happened historically in those countries that have not followed the one true God.

How will we, as individuals, escape from being declared the Lord's enemies if we vote to elect officials who hold positions contrary to what our Lord teaches? We are responsible in a democracy! We can try to dodge responsibility by claiming that our leaders did this or our leaders did that, but we, the voters, elected them and put them in office. If we voted for them without knowing their beliefs, then we must accept that responsibility. If we know the candidates' beliefs and positions and support them, even when we know them to be inconsistent with God's laws, then we have directly opposed God, and we are again responsible.

God speaks to this in his word, and even though the word "hypocrisy" is used only a couple of times, the theme of hypocrisy is rampant throughout the Bible. Consider these two passages in God's word:

Luke 6:46–49: *"Why do you call me, 'Lord, Lord,' and do not do what I say? I will show you what he is like who comes to me and hears my words and puts them into practice. He is like a man building a house, who dug down deep and laid the foundation on rock. When a flood came, the torrent struck that house but could not shake it, because it was well built. But the one who hears my words and does not put them into practice is like a man who built a house on the ground without a foundation. The moment the torrent struck that house, it collapsed and its destruction was complete."*

Matthew 7:21–27: *"Not everyone who says to me, 'Lord, Lord,' will enter the kingdom of heaven, but only he who does the will of my Father who is in heaven. Many will say to me on that day, 'Lord, Lord, did we not prophesy in your name and in your name drive out demons and perform many miracles?' Then I will tell them plainly, 'I never knew you. Away from me you evildoers!' Therefore, everyone who hears these words of mine and puts them into practice is like a wise man who built his house on the rock. The rain came down, the streams rose, and the winds blew and beat against that house; yet it did not fall, because it had its foundation on the rock. But everyone who hears these words of mine and does not put them into practice is like a foolish man who built his house on sand. The rain came down, the streams rose, and the winds blew and beat against that house, and it fell with a great crash."*

Ask yourself these questions:

- Am I obeying God when I vote for or support candidates who endorse abortion?

- Am I obeying God when I vote for or support candidates who support separation of church and state by eliminating God-centric decision making and acknowledgment of God?

- Am I obeying God when I vote for or support candidates who support honoring false gods?

- Am I obeying God when I vote for or support candidates who espouse a platform of peace at any cost?

- Am I obeying God when I vote for or support candidates who appoint judges who will not punish the guilty, who deny justice to the victims, and who fail to protect potential victims?

- Am I obeying God when I vote for or support judges who reject God and his authority over my life?

- Am I obeying God when I vote for or support candidates who advocate premarital sex or support child sexuality?

- Am I obeying God when I vote for or support candidates who support homosexuality or same-sex marriage?

- Am I obeying God when I vote for or support candidates who steal from the American people by being financially irresponsible or by spending hard-working Americans' Social Security money?

- Am I obeying God when I vote for or support candidates who are not opposed to pornography and the exploitation of men and women?

- Am I obeying God when I vote for or support candidates who show favoritism to those who have made huge contributions to their campaigns?

- Am I obeying God when I vote for or support candidates who don't have the courage to do what is right in God's sight?

- Am I obeying God when I vote for or support candidates who spend money that this country does not have, especially for things this country does not need?

We must decide whether we are going to obey the God of the Bible by using his commands as a foundation for this country which it traditionally has been, or whether we are going to set our own laws, regardless of whether they contradict God's commands.

It is surprising how many of the things we do in this country are directly opposed to God's commands. Here is a simple example: Our kids are literally under attack. A major TV network, NBC through its sting operations, has had no problem ensnaring adults who are seeking to have sex with underage kids they have met on the Internet. Judges often refuse to punish those convicted of sexual crimes against minors which may have resulted in the death of a 12 year old in Vermont. Listen to what God has to say about this very topic:

Proverbs 17:15: *Acquitting the guilty and condemning the innocent— the LORD detests them both.*

Proverbs 24:24–25: *Whoever says to the guilty, "You are innocent"—peoples will curse him and nations denounce him. But it will go well with those who convict the guilty, and rich blessing will come upon them.*

God does love us, but this love has never stopped him from punishing those who are committed to doing wrong (according to his standard, not ours). We punish our children when they do wrong, even though we love them, and our God is no different. Furthermore, as parents we do not have unlimited tolerance for our children's disobedience. Neither does God. This is why the Bible correctly says that fear of God is the beginning of knowledge. If we do not fear and respect someone who has the ability to punish us, we tend to gravitate back toward our sinful nature.

Politicians all across this land attend church and claim to follow God and then turn around and espouse ungodly positions. Who are these people? According to the Bible, they are liars, yet these are the people we are electing to lead our country. We are directly responsible when we elect them and do not hold them accountable.

1 John 2:2–4: *We know that we have come to know him if we obey his commands. The man who says, "I know him," but does not do what he commands is a liar, and the truth is not in him.*

It is important to be clear that God does not endorse our taking vengeance on those who reject God and his commands. We do not create specific laws to punish those who are homosexual, but we must not institute a single law that enables or supports such a lifestyle, and we must counsel them to leave their lives of sin. To show any level of support would be contradicting the laws of God, and we will be held responsible for that. Our laws should mirror God's laws.

Please, America; come to study the very words of God so that you can know what pleases him and what angers him, and then make decisions on issues and candidates that are consistent with what God commands. If we do not do this, we are doomed. God's mercy does have limits. Consider the words of God to Jerusalem:

Ezekiel 14:12–23: *The word of the LORD came to me: Son of man, if a country sins against me by being unfaithful and I stretch out my hand against it to cut off its food supply and send famine upon it and kill its men and their animals, even if these three men—Noah, Daniel, and Job—were in it, they could save only themselves by their righteousness, declares the*

Sovereign LORD. Or if I send wild beasts through that country and they leave it childless and it becomes desolate so that no one can pass through it because of the beasts, as surely as I live, declares the Sovereign LORD, even if these three men were in it, they could not save their own sons or daughters. They alone would be saved, but the land would be desolate. Or if I bring a sword against that country and say, Let the sword pass throughout the land, and I kill its men and their animals, as surely as I live, declares the Sovereign LORD, even if these three men were in it, they could not save their own sons or daughters. They alone would be saved. Or if I send a plague into that land and pour out my wrath upon it through bloodshed, killing its men and their animals, as surely as I live, declares the Sovereign LORD, even if Noah, Daniel and Job were in it, they could save neither son nor daughter. They would save only themselves by their righteousness. For this is what the Sovereign LORD says: How much worse will it be when I send against Jerusalem my four dreadful judgments—sword and famine and wild beasts and plague—to kill its men and their animals! Yet there will be some survivors—sons and daughters who will be brought out of it. They will come to you, and when you see their conduct and their actions, you will be consoled regarding the disaster I have brought upon Jerusalem—every disaster I have brought upon it. You will be consoled when you see their conduct and their actions, for you will know that I have done nothing in it without cause, declares the Sovereign LORD.

When we enter into the most dire of times in our existence, we will know that the Lord has acted with cause. It is our steadfast refusal to submit to his laws that will be our undoing.

Democracy on a Firm Foundation

The United States is a democracy, but the reason that is has stood and prospered for so long is because this country was founded on godly principles, and its people have worshipped the one and only living God—the God of the Bible. God has rescued this country from large numbers of events that have plagued other parts of the world, and we have been blessed. We have traditionally created and enacted laws based on God's commands and now the pillars upon which this country has traditionally stood are starting to erode. And with the erosion of these godly pillars, the foundation of the country itself is starting to crumble.

There are many people in this country who lead a lifestyle that is in defiance of God's commands; through through their selfish demands, they reject God. Many will dismiss the information in this book as religious dogma, not believing in an absolute truth but accepting all religions and denying the fundamental truth: there is only one truth. Others will dismiss this book, preferring instead to believe in a long string of cosmic coincidences and denying the existence of any God.

Others, however, will hear God's voice and know what is presented here to be true. Some of them will be motivated to action. Some of them will remain passive and take no action, even though they acknowledge the correctness of what is presented here. Whatever your situation, please consider the words of this book as you cast your vote for your elected officials. If we cannot find the will to do what is right, we will suffer for doing what is wrong. What will your response be to the call to do what is right, to hold accountable those who lead this country?

Will you get involved? Will you ensure that you understand God's will and compare leaders' beliefs and actions against that will?

So what do we do when we are presented with a series of candidates, none of whom operates consistent with godly principles? This is a tough question and one that I have personally wrestled with. I believe that we initially must work through our political process to ensure that we get godly leaders by supporting those who truly believe in God and act accordingly, but if that process should fail us, we have little choice but to support the godliest candidate we can. Remember that we all fail God from time to time, but we should still seek candidates who do the most conscientious jobs of acknowledging God and seek to follow his laws. If the leader we select is ungodly, God himself can replace him. My conviction is that if we truly seek God, he will help us by providing godly leaders.

I know that many will argue with this position, saying that we live in a democracy and majority rules, but this democracy has stood longer than any other in the world because its foundation *was* God. We must strive to return to that foundation and ensure that we do not make laws inconsistent with God's commands. We must not continue to pass and enact ungodly laws. We cannot let a minority of individuals lead us down the path of destruction, simply because many of the rest of us are too apathetic to oppose those who rely on an immoral framework thatoften is based on no more than their feelings.

This county is slowly but surely turning into a modern-day Sodom and Gomorrah, and if we don't change, its end will be no different. Why do we undertake these types of actions? It is because we have rejected God and because we do not accept his sovereignty over our lives. We took the freedom that was afforded us by God and used it to do evil in his sight. Some of the sins above are committed on an individual basis, and some sins have been legitimized through the judicial process, but no matter how we look at it, we make the laws through our legal process. We, as a people, are responsible for the laws under which we live.

Although God said the following to Israel, my conviction is that it applies to the United States as well. God knew that many countries would forsake him and worship other gods (and we do this, although we may not think of them as gods, per se). Read the following passage in Deuteronomy 28:1–52 carefully. Does any of this sound familiar? Note the various pieces of this passage.

If you fully obey the LORD your God and carefully follow all his commands I give you today, the LORD your God will set you high above all the nations on earth.… The LORD your God will bless you in the land he is giving you…The LORD will grant you abundant prosperity—in the fruit of your womb, the young of your livestock and the crops of your ground—in the land he swore to your forefathers to give you. The LORD will open the heavens, the storehouse of his bounty, to send rain on your land in season and to bless all the work of your hands. You will lend to many nations but will borrow from none.. The LORD will make you the head, not the tail. If you pay attention to the commands of the LORD your God that I give you this day and carefully follow them, you will always be at the top, never at the bottom. Do not turn aside from any of the commands I give you today, to the right or to the left, following other gods and serving them.…..However, if you do not obey the LORD your God and do not carefully follow all his commands and decrees I am giving you today, all these curses will come upon you and overtake you: …You will be unsuccessful in everything you do; day after day you will be oppressed and robbed, with no one to rescue you. Your sons and daughters will be given to another nation, and you will wear out your eyes watching for them day after day, powerless to lift a hand. …The alien who lives among you will rise above you higher and higher, but you will sink lower and lower. He will lend to you, but you will not lend to him.….. He will be the head, but you will be the tail. All these curses will come upon you. …The LORD will bring a nation against you from far away, from the ends of the earth, like an eagle swooping down, a nation whose language you will not understand, a fierce-looking nation without respect for the old or pity for the young.

We are in a difficult position. We want to trust our leaders and yet they govern from the wrong vantage point, either because they cannot perceive the truth or because they reject the truth of God. Because they cannot accept the truth, they govern in the manner they see fit or as they are influenced by others. The more honorable individuals in public service attempt to represent their constituents accurately but often, they operate without having the necessary basis of truth to effectively guide their decision making.

Others are interested in seeking to fulfill their own personal agendas. Consider congressional lawmakers who have squandered our Social Security funds. One recent candidate even suggested raising taxes as a way to cover the funds that they have squandered. Add to this the extra-marital affairs, the pandering to those who espouse hate, the lack of self control, the legislation introduced directly opposing the positions of the majority of Americans (e.g. abortion, homosexuality), representing special-interest groups rather than the American public, and the attempts at eliminating God from government, and you have leadership which will destroy this country.

Although this is a democracy, we still cannot tolerate ungodly practices or laws. There is still a basic morality that must be maintained, even in a democracy, and this basic morality is the God-given morality—those tenets that we cannot deny or change, even if the majority wants to change them. We have no right to change that which God has commanded, and because we are subject to his power, we need to recognize this and submit to his will in these matters.

Now, please don't misunderstand—this is not a call for revolution. It is a call to vote only for those individuals who are committed to governing according to the truth of the God of the Bible. Our Founding Fathers risked their lives to establish this country based on biblical principles. We must have the integrity to cling to these same tenets if this country is to survive.

We have become so apathetic to the way in which they lead that unless it affects us personally, we don't act.

Those who have the least will pay for it most, but we will all suffer. We are as guilty as our leaders in accepting lifestyles that are ungodly, rather than rejecting them. We simply must stop living with indifference to God's laws. If we refuse to do so, our destruction will be on our own heads. Here are the top ten things (in no particular order) that we do that are clearly ungodly:

- We pass laws allowing for abortion.

- We pass laws enabling homosexual life-styles.

- We tolerate adultery and sex outside of marriage.

- We do not administer justice in a godly way.

- We acknowledge other religions as acceptable, even though they embody false gods and false beliefs.

- We are racist.

- We are too materialistic.

- We lie.

- We ignore the plight of poor.

- We do not love God first and foremost.

Once we begin to address these things and acknowledge God's ways as correct, then we will have a chance to have this country blessed again and perhaps God will relent and not bring the destruction that we have been asking for.

I will acknowledge that there are many issues that arise about which the Bible does not directly communicate a position. Such issues include the level of taxation, the laws on alcohol, whether the county should go to war, etc. These are the more disputable matters, and I am not here to address these, although more often than not, there are underlying tenets or teachings from which one can determine God's will on a given issue. We need not worry about every potential issue. Let's at least focus on getting the basics right, and then we can worry about the more debatable issues before us. If we cannot even stop the murder of babies or stop our homosexual practices, what chance do we have to understand the more complex issues?

Tragedies have affected our people (the shootings at Columbine and Virginia Tech, the horror of 9/11, etc.), and we have asked "Where is God?" Are we crazy? We support homosexuality, which God outlaws, and then when pure evil shows up in our culture, we ask "Where is God?" We simply cannot expect God to answer our prayers and come to our defense when we reject his laws and commands. We are hypocritical in that we expect him to be there for us when we are not there for him. Teachers in our schools teach immorality, directly against what God teaches, and then when a young person commits mass murder in school, we ask "Why?" It is because we have taught our own kids all too well that God's morals don't matter. We watch as teachers espouse their own morals, and the very kids they teach begin to understand that they also can craft their own morality, and use it, at times, to deadly effect. We are crafting a culture that is ungodly, and there is only one group of people that will pay for it—us! Other nations have fallen into this trap, but let's not follow their example.

I understand this is a democracy, but we need to have a strong set of moral values to which the democracy adheres, and these are being eroded every day, primarily by those who do not know God or his commands. If we do not keep these, we will be destroyed. There are still plenty of issues on which we can debate and allow the majority to rule, but our fundamental tenets and truths must be obtained from God and nowhere else.

WHAT WE MUST DO

Our time in this country is running out. The time to act is now. If we fail to act, if we fail to confront evil, if we fail to hold our leaders accountable for not doing what is right, if we fail to hold our leaders accountable for not accurately representing the people, then it is we will bear the consequences. The responsibility for our failures however does not exist solely with the leaders that we elect. We share some of responsibility for our problems.

We listen and follow leaders who promise us things they cannot deliver, and we accept those promises, even though they are too good to be true. We elect leaders who either are too naïve to understand the implications of what they promise us or who are deceitful, as they know full well the implications of what they promise. Witness the Social Security system, the funds of which have been effectively plundered by our leaders, all while ensuring the integrity of their own retirement packages. If we keep on only electing those who promise us good things, we will destroy this country. We need leaders who follow the truth as established by God, not those who seek their own glory by promising us what we want to hear as a means to gain power. We need leaders who will represent the American people accurately and not just the few individuals who invest large amounts of resources lining the coffers of the candidates and leaders they support. We are moving away from a democracy and moving towards rule by rich as our leaders fail to pass and enforce laws consistent with the American peoples' wills. Surveys show, that at least for now, that the American people want a godly government and preservation of our society. Heaven help us when we turn our backs on God, but for right now the American people have shown they want God in their government and guiding our decisions.

Consider the laws passed by our government and yet look at what six surveys conducted by American Solutions surveys reveal in terms of what the American public wants (contrasted with what our leaders are doing to us). Each of these surveys has a statistical error of 3%-4%.

- 82% of Americans do NOT want prayer banned in schools (and yet we have laws and schools which enforce such restrictions)

- 87% of Americans want English as the official language (but our leaders will not affirm this with legislation)

- 83% of Americans believe immigrants should be required to learn English (yet we continue to pass legislation requiring at huge cost, usage of other languages)

- 68% believe that the United States should grant citizenship only to those who want to embrace American values and culture (and yet our leaders are shifting our values towards other cultures)

- 86% believe that statements made regarding religion and morality made by the founding fathers are just important today as they were more than 200 years ago (and yet we are trying to eliminate the one true God from our society)

- 88% believe that illegal immigrants who commit felonies should be deported (and yet there are sanctuary cities that flaunt the rule of law by protecting such individuals)

- 78% believe that our dependence on foreign oil threatens our economic prosperity (and yet we are seeing the greatest transference of wealth in history from America to other nations, some of who have a significant percentage of their populace willing to give their lives to kill us)

- 69% believe the existing federal income tax structure is unfair (and yet our leaders will not change it)

- 88% believe that keeping the reference to "One Nation Under God" in the Pledge of Allegiance is very important (and yet we have judges in the Ninth Federal Circuit Court who support its removal)

- 81% of Americans believe that separation of church and state does not mean that no references to God in government sanctioned activities or public buildings should be present (yet we have organizations (ex. ACLU) who find sympathetic ears in our judges and political leaders seeking to remove this influence)

- 85% of Americans feel that Iran poses a serious threat to the United States (yet we have an astounding level of naivety by believing that we can win over extremists with talk)

- 65% of Americans believe that many of the problems our country faces is because America is no longer as religious and moral as it once was and NOT a result of changes in the economy, war, public education and other issues (and yet we have our leaders trying to drive us even further away from God's standard of morality).

We must start holding our leaders accountable to what the American public wants and not the philosophies of a few well to do individuals.

We also must be willing to hear the bad news (i.e., the truth) from truthful leaders and not listen to the errant promises of politicians who cannot deliver. We must realize that far too many of us have lived a life of overindulgence, while many around the world starve. We have borrowed money beyond our ability to repay it. We must turn back to sound moral and financial principles. To this end, we must ensure that we elect leaders who are committed to telling truth, however hard that may be, and who are committed to doing the will of God and using his values as the basis of the laws they enact and the decisions they make. We cannot hide behind the veil of political correctness or give in to individuals who, although charismatic, have no conviction to stand up for what is right. The primary deciding factor for a leader must be shifted back to doing what is right, using God's word as the standard.

It does not mean that people who follow such beliefs cannot be in our nation. What it does mean is that we need to maintain our standard of right and wrong, regardless of who enters this country, regardless of what influence those living in this country succumb to. We must not tire of doing what is right and must stand up for those values. Just as English should be our official language and those coming into this country should be required to respect it and learn it, the same should exist for our value system. If those in this country don't like the rules of our Creator, they can leave. Does this seem intolerant? Perhaps so, but the outcomes of their way of living will cause us all great harm.

We, as a country, cannot be all things to all people if we are to survive as a country. This means that we cannot both support and oppose abortion. We cannot support and oppose homosexuality. We must select one path, and the path that we select must be based on our Creator's values and not simply the values we as a nation find convenient. There are those who will claim the Bible is not clear on many issues, but we are enacting laws that are inconsistent with the clear teachings of the Bible. Let us focus on getting the basics right before we start worrying about the more esoteric issues. The truth is the truth, and we must stand for that truth. We must not be apathetic to those who oppose the truth and not allow ourselves to be carried away with alternate truths, which are no truths at all.

For God said in Jeremiah 7, *"Therefore say to them, 'This is the nation that has not obeyed the LORD its God or responded to correction. Truth has perished; it has vanished from their lips."* We are becoming that same nation in that there are so many individuals espousing their versions of the truth that we have a hard time telling the truth from fiction. This should not be so! Let us return to the truth as espoused by our God!

The key here is that we must be willing to stand up for what is right and not allow those who want anything to exert their influence over us. If they do not like the rules in this country, they can leave—they have that freedom. We must not allow them to try to influence us to get us to accept that which is wrong.

We, as individuals in a democracy, must start holding ourselves and our leaders accountable. Those who have abandoned God, in one form or another, will be directly responsible for ruining this country, if we allow them to. God has blessed us in many ways, but the arrogance of those who do not believe that God has provided the blessings are only angering the God who has blessed us. Do not submit to their lies, immoral activities, or personal agendas. Instead, let us submit to the Lord, who has blessed this country greatly. Remember that we have many years of experience with the Lord's blessings. Why would we allow those who refuse to give God the glory for those blessings lead us away from God?

I would propose that any individual running for political office in the United States be held accountable to the "American Pledge" which would ask him to state his support or rejection of it. I have assembled this based on the teachings of God in the Bible. It does not venture into disputable matters. It uses the teachings of God "as is." I realize there will be all sorts of people who will try technical evasions to get around these declarations, but these evasions do not stand the test of God's word and his standard of right and wrong. We cannot let those running for office and serving in office lead us into accepting ungodly positions on issues.

Furthermore, we must be willing to recall politicians who will not submit to God's laws and try to enact laws that are inconsistent with the teachings of God. We have to get involved to save this nation. We cannot be apathetic to the sin of this nation any longer, nor can we let those who cannot distinguish right from wrong (according to God's word) lead us as a nation. If we allow this, we will all suffer.

The American Pledge is below. We must hold our leaders accountable to this set of morals if we want leaders who can truly lead this country where it needs to go and can help us avoid the oncoming crisis.

The American Elected and Appointed Official Pledge

I, _____, either running for or appointed to any political office or position of judge, agree that I will:

Acknowledge the Bible as the standard of right and wrong and will make decisions and laws consistent with its teachings;

Not support abortion and will seek to outlaw abortion, the killing of innocent children;

Not pass laws which support homosexuality in any form;

Adopt the principles of sound financial management as defined by the Bible, including moving the United States away from being a debtor nation;

(For political officials) Put the needs of my constituents before myself and accurately represent the entire counsel of my constituency according to democratic principles;

(For judges) Will judge fairly, including punishing those who violate the law in a manner consistent with their crimes and protecting others;

Seek to ensure that the God of the Bible can be recognized in what this county does, inclusive of public venues such as schools, governmental offices, and public proceedings;

Not take money or influence from lobbyists, political action groups, or others individuals or groups seeking to advance a specific agenda.

In the event that I violate these commitments to the American public, I shall resign my position as a political official or judge.

Signed _____

Dated _____

Does such a doctrine seem corny to you? My friends, this is no joke. Let us avoid the mistake of provoking our God to anger by supporting further rebellion against him. We are not without hope yet. God in Jeremiah 18 says, *"If at any time I announce that a nation or kingdom is to be uprooted, torn down, and destroyed, and if that nation I warned repents of its evil, then I will relent and not inflict on it the disaster I had planned."*

Countrymen and countrywomen, I implore you to consider these words. My only motive in writing this book is to call us back to God so that we might spare our children and our children's children the evil legacy we currently are leaving them. It is God's morals that matter and his commands that we must respect. If we cannot muster the courage and the will to obey God, then we and all future generations will suffer.

May God open your hearts to this message as you seek his will.

A FINAL MESSAGE

Countrymen and countrywomen, we are all going to die someday and where we spend eternity will depend on the choices we make in this life. You cannot live a good enough life to be saved without Jesus Christ and if you simply look at God's word, it will be clear that we have all sinned against God in some form or another. Jesus paid the price for our sin and only through his sacrifice can we avoid eternal damnation, avoiding the penalty for our sin. This is God's plan for our salvation.

Friends, there is only one way to God and that is through his son, Jesus Christ. I know there are many religions in the world and that it is politically uncomfortable to not accept them, but if you look into it, you will quickly realize they cannot all be true. In fact, there is only one truth, and the diversity in the teachings of many religions testifies that most must be false. The truth is contained in the Bible—the only document that bears God's testimony and evidence to support it. Religions based on subsequent documents and testimonies must be tested against the Bible to see if those documents are true or false. God has told us through his word that he has spoken to us in these last days through his son so that we might not be carried away with all other "false" revelations.

To those of you who may not know the Lord Jesus Christ, I want to tell you that there is a God who loves you, who sent his only son to pay the debt for the sins we have committed against our God. It is he who will be waiting to meet each of us after we die. Our God demands justice for our sin, but through the sacrifice of his son, Jesus, he has satisfied his justice for our sin and extended mercy to us. This is the *only* provision he has made for extending mercy, allowing us to avoid the penalty of our sin. We cannot do enough good works to cover the sin we have committed. We will all stand before him and be judged, but Jesus is our mediator, and even though our verdict has already been determined as guilty, the penalty for the sin has already been paid. We need only accept and follow Jesus. Look objectively at your own life. Have you lied? Have you looked at another man or woman lustfully? Have you ever stolen anything? Have you ever gotten drunk? There are so many different sins. None of us can stand before the Lord and claim to be righteous, yet it is our sins that separate us from God. Jesus—and only Jesus—can bridge that gulf, if you accept him as your savior.

If you do not know Christ, please take this opportunity to give yourself to Jesus and seek him through his word. Save yourselves from this corrupt generation by placing your entire faith in Jesus and submitting to his will. Get baptized, join a church, and serve the living God. May God bless you individually as you accept Christ as your Lord—and the United States as a country—as we seek God's will and not our own.